Acknowledgements

My deepest gratitude is to my mom and dad for their commitment to us children. Despite all hardship, they modeled a deep integrity. I hope they are smiling up there as I birth this book. I so appreciate my brothers and sisters for their respect and support.

To my teachers, I thank you. It took a village to convince me that I had something valuable to contribute. Paul Romer, my first mentor, taught me how to use my own breath to experience my divinity. Janet Mentgen, creator of the Healing Touch Program, accelerated my own healing with her expertise in energy medicine. Tim and Barbara Cook taught me contemplative prayer, which healed a lot of my childhood trauma. The faculty at University of Spiritual Healing & Sufism enriched my life with the Remembrance, a practice that helped me to discover my own heart.

To all the babies I have held - the numbers are now in the thousands! You are my teachers as well, reminding me of purity and innocence.

A special thanks to Barbara Starke, Sharon Scandrett-Hibdon, Alex Palomo, Amina Al-Jamal, and Randy Peyser for reading my manuscript and giving me feedback, to Nancy Bryan for her proofreading, to my very special friends for the beautiful cover photo, and to Nicole and Bill for the pictures of their son Jude.

To my current coaches Michelle Price and Suzy Prudden, if it weren't for you, this book would still be in my computer.

I express deep thanks to all those who have participated in my healing, so many that it would take a whole book to thank those who helped me hope and dared me to dream. I have had a long road home to myself, and have finally accepted the fact that you don't have to be perfect to teach, and that often we get the privilege of teaching what we need to learn.

Dedication

This book is dedicated to babies everywhere.

May they receive the best start possible in life.

This is also dedicated to the baby within each one of us.

May we all

remember.

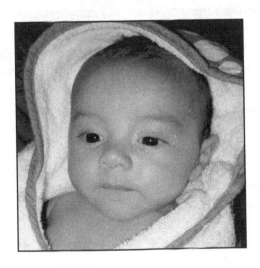

Reviews and Comments

Your Baby Remembers will hopefully someday become required reading for every pregnant woman and parent of a newborn and infant. From the unique perspective of her many years spent in the newborn intensive care nursery, this highly compassionate and intuitive nurse has written a work of art from her heart. Filled with practical and insightful suggestions for caring and connecting with your baby, Rita Kluny has provided mothers with a wonderful gift - a 21st century guide to creating an exceptional start in life for your child.

Dr. Rob Ivker, DO, ABIHM

Co-founder and Past-president, American Board of Integrative Holistic Medicine, Author, *Sinus Survival,*

Past President, American Holistic Medical Association

Your Baby Remembers is truly inspirational. As a licensed clinical psychologist, I see the effect in my practice of suffering that stems from problems in bonding between parents and children. This neonatal intensive care nurse presents a moving description of her journey of personal healing. She teaches how love is healing for one's self and infants. The most vulnerable infants and the most frightened parents are offered hope and healing. I strongly and enthusiastically recommend this book. Psychology posits the presence of an inner child in all of us. Rita Kluny provides a road map of how to heal the inner child through remembering our connection to divine love. The story is true. I know, because I had the distinct pleasure of meeting the author. The spiritual practices featured can lead to significant and lasting benefits in one's life. Especially if you are a parent, it can help you to from fear, helplessness, lack of connection to a greater sense of peace, joy, love and mastery. Do yourself a favor, read this book and share it with an expectant mother to be.

Randy Levine, Ph.D. Licensed Clinical Psychologist

The most important healing in the world today is with our babies. Rita takes us on her journey of touching the lives and hearts of babies and parents creating acceptance of who they are.... perfect and loved. Rita weaves her life around unconditional love for all who are entering our world, healing herself and others along the way. She is a dedicated nurse and angel to all she touches with her gifts and we are blessed beyond measure for her life.

Judy Matejczyk
President, *I Am A Miracle* Foundation

When I first read this amazing book my first thoughts were how much I wanted to get to know the author – Rita Kluny. In my mind anyone who spoke so gently and confidently about love and the powerful balm it is for us and our children was a person I wanted in my life. I have been blessed to spend time with Rita. She is truly authentic in her beliefs. Her teaching is based on years of personal experience and is a great gift for any mother at any stage of motherhood. This book brings to light the miracle of life and how connected each of us are. The beautiful flow of love from parent to child is a never-ending process of giving and receiving. Although my son now has a son of his own, I have learned from Rita that the power of love has no age limit or physical boundary. It is essence and with our willingness to give and receive this love - our life is healed and healing is offered to all. Thank you Rita. My most sincere wishes for the successful distribution of this much needed book.

Mary D. Bolen, Licensed Unity Teacher & Spiritual Counselor
Unity Church of the Hills, Austin, TX

About the Author

Rita has been teaching Healing Touch since 1993, and is certified in HT as an instructor and practitioner. She is certified in Holistic Nursing, and was honored as the 1994 American Holistic Nurse of the Year. She introduced Healing Touch into Omega Institute for Holistic Studies' Wellness Center, where she spent seven seasons giving private sessions to staff and workshop attendees of all ages.

Rita has spent decades as a nurse in Neonatal intensive Care. Her deep desire is that babies have the opportunity for the best start in life. She has two visions: first is to see Healing Touch integrated into pre and perinatal care, and second is to empower moms to experience the value of self care and prenatal bonding during pregnancy. Rita provides support through www.yourbabyremembers.com, an educational and experiential website for pregnant or new moms and dads.

Rita is a member of American Holistic Nurses Association, Healing Touch Professional Associates, and the Association for Pre&Perinatal Psychology and Health. She has written many articles on healing, some of which you can find in the archives of Energy Magazine. She is a contributor in the new *Healing Touch Guidebook, Chicken Soup for the Nurse's Soul, 1st edition,* and featured in the book *Nurse Healers.*

Your Baby Remembers is her first book.

Foreword

Rita Kluny offers us a gem with her book, *Your Baby Remembers*. A neonatal intensive care nurse, she describes groundbreaking research on the prenatal experience and the impact of the parent-child relationship on the developing baby in the womb. This fascinating body of research is transforming much of what we thought we knew about babies in the womb. Babies and newborns are much more aware and impacted by their environment, including parental emotions both positive and negative, than previously believed. Instead of blaming parents, Rita looks compassionately at this phenomenon and offers a beautiful, gentle, meditative healing practice to bring more love, peace, and harmony into the lives and relationships of parents and babies. Along the way, she shares her own personal journey of healing, from the Peace Corps to Findhorn and back to neonatal nursing. With every page, I thought of more and more people that I wanted to share this information with. Parents-to-be will find it especially useful in helping them to build a strong and loving bond with their unborn babies, even before birth, but everyone who's ever been a parent or a baby will find this book intriguing and healing.

Dr. Elizabeth Ihsan Rose, Ph.D., Psychologist
Faculty, University of Spiritual Healing and Sufism

Table of Contents

Preface

Are we failing our children? Most women live fast, complex lives managing careers, raising families, keeping food on the table, and worrying about the economy. Families have turned into individuals who live under the same roof, yet spend little meaningful or loving time with one another. In fact, most mothers spend the majority of their time in a constant state of stress as they juggle their schedules and race to stay on top of it all. Meanwhile, many children feel neglected or disconnected. Low self-esteem in children is rampant. It then comes as no surprise that they are turning to drugs, gangs, violence, and suicide at ages that are too young to fathom.

Your Baby Remembers: Parenting with a Deep Heart from the Start, introduces moms and moms-to-be to a new form of prenatal preparation that can help prevent (or heal) the disconnection that is happening all too frequently between mothers and their children. Most people think that the wounding and disconnection that children experience begins at puberty, but actually it originates much earlier in life, often prior to birth.

The October 2010 cover article of TIME Magazine introduced the field of Fetal Origins. Science has determined that whatever happens during pregnancy can affect the health of babies for the rest of their lives. This is important information to grasp, to realize that pregnancy itself involves conscious effort to secure the best start in life for a baby.

Your Baby Remembers includes research revealing that babies are sentient beings who need love, connection and communication from their parents to help formulate a cellular memory of safety and trust as their bodies are forming in utero. Babies are imprinted with their mothers' cellular structure. They take on their attributes, even those that are forgotten, hidden, buried in old stories. Suppressed memories and painful experiences can be passed on to the baby unless cellular memory is erased beforehand. When a woman becomes aware of the parts of herself that need healing, she creates a clear foundation for her relationship with her child, and strengthens her ability to parent from the heart. Her baby can be free from familial patterns that were painful.

Newborn babies carry awareness that can be healing for a family. I relate this in two ways: by citing neurobiological research and by sharing my own direct experience of looking back into the past to understand my own beginnings.

Mothers need to know that the physiology of Love itself can be altered by the medicalization of the birthing process. Instead of birth empowering women to transition into motherhood, it has morphed into a procedure whereby women are having birth done to them. When nature does not take its course during the birthing process, the connection between mother and child can be altered, even diluted. This dilution of the mother/child bond may not be obvious at the time. Most moms don't realize that something deeply organic went missing in their birth experience. If recognized early, it can be addressed and healed.

Your Baby Remembers is intended to revolutionize how a mom relates to her baby. With loving attention, she can build her baby's self esteem from conception. *Your Baby Remembers* is meant to inspire moms to realize the importance of relaxation and stress management to ensure a healthier, more intelligent baby.

Everyone knows the damage stress can create. Most people are overloaded with the problem aspect, but few are aware of the solution for both parent and child. Later in the book, I describe a study done by a Hungarian obstetrician who taught his prenatal patients a practice of prenatal bonding. His patients learned to communicate with their unborn babies. This had profound effects on the birthing process. Complications were rare. Not one mother had postpartum depression! Intentional prenatal contact was apparently mutually beneficial

Times are complex and troubled. There is so much distraction from the outside world, that women neglect their bodies and their inner world. *Your Baby Remembers* reminds mothers that pregnancy is a crucial time to invest in themselves. By discovering and nurturing their own inner sanctuary, they can help to keep their children intact. They may not be able to save them from painful experiences, but they can transmit safety and trust, helping them to stay true to themselves as they grow older.

How would a child's life, or the bond between a mother and child, be affected if expecting parents would

1) Realize that the chronic stress mom experiences can create stress patterns in her baby that might lead to lower IQ or ill health.
2) Be aware that their baby's memories are recorded even prior to brain development.
3) Invest time during pregnancy, birth, and the postpartum period to transform their own emotional patterns, so that their baby would be free of them.
4) Slow down enough to truly receive the miracle and beauty of creation.

This book does not focus on what is wrong with families, but rather on keeping the family holy or whole. The bottom line is to realize that babies are conscious, sentient beings who already possess sophisticated awareness and understanding. *And that memory starts at conception.*

I invite you to become an empowered parent from the very beginning. When the connection runs deep, the bond cannot be broken. My intention is to help parents heal their own pain and suffering, so that they can truly celebrate their baby, be reminded of their own innocence, and radiate that purity and Light out into the world.

Chapter 1

My Intention for the Reader

As a registered nurse, I see a lot of pain in the Neonatal Intensive Care Unit (NICU): premature babies born too soon, parents longing to take their babies home. If these moms had been fortunate enough to practice prenatal bonding, perhaps some of these situations could have been prevented, or at least alleviated. Rather than suffering a crisis, they might be celebrating taking their new baby home. My passion is to offer this information, along with my own methodology, to help parents give their babies the greatest potential for the best start possible.

My personal story is so intricately intertwined with this process, that I feel compelled to share my background. I have always loved babies. Their world is delicate, vibrant and mysterious. We think we don't remember our own infancy, yet it lives deeply buried in our sensations and body memories. Perhaps this is why babies are captivating. They are like magnets. We want to touch them, look at them, play with them. Babies often create a bridge between adults, who connect by talking about them. Everyone notices a pregnant woman. A friend once said that she felt invisible to the human race, until she was pregnant. Then everyone wanted to talk to her, to relate to the world of baby, to new life.

What gets so deeply stirred in us when we look into a newborn's eyes? Are we suddenly facing something inside us that is also fresh and whole? Are we remembering our original state? Are we reminded of our own painful beginnings?

A spiritual mentor of mine said that the reason I work with babies is to heal my own inner infant. That is really true. I grew up with babies, helping my mom with my younger brother and sister. After graduating from college, I started working in the Neonatal Intensive Care. I loved their innocence, and it was easy for me to care for these delicate patients. No matter how premature they were, no matter how small, each one already had a unique personality.

I became a nurse at a time when the medical world assumed that babies felt no pain, so there was little attempt at pain management. I often wondered if they would remember their own rough beginnings: prolonged separation from their mothers, isolation in incubators, and painful medical procedures. I did not delve deeply into these issues at that time; I found it too depressing. We often discharged babies who were born too soon, who would perhaps be blind from oxygen complications, deaf from strong antibiotics, have learning disabilities, and might suffer from cerebral palsy as well. What hurt the most was how much we focused on the physical, and how little emotional support we gave the parents.

It bothered me so much that, after four years in nursing, I joined the Peace Corps. I found tremendous value, living in other cultures, and traveling all over the world. Leaving the familiar was not easy, but it gave me a frame of reference to who we are as a society, how we value our children, and how birth is experienced. I saw how much more medicalized our country was around birth and how much more bonded children were with their parents in Third World countries. I witnessed many natural births performed by community midwives. Women found their strength, and became empowered in the birthing process. Despite near poverty, their lives felt more organic, more connected.

After my two-year tour, I traveled for a year in South America. My desire for adventure started to wane, so I returned to the States, but felt lost. Life had sped up and I had slowed down. The pace was unsettling. I felt little in common with my own culture. I worked long enough to save money to leave again. I was yearning to understand myself. My focus became introspective. I traveled to Findhorn, a healing community in Scotland. It was intriguing to discover the healing arts. In between the classes and workshops, I mingled with people from all over the world who had the common goal of finding something within themselves that they had lost or forgotten, be it heart, soul, Spirit, or all of the above. Originally, I planned to stay two weeks but I could not leave, it was so very healing, My intention was that my next step would reveal itself before I left, and that took longer than I thought!

I met a clairvoyant from Los Angeles. She asked me about myself, and I was eager to share. She held my hand while she listened to me, then, she simply said, "You need to try Rebirthing. It would be really good for you."

I had no idea what that was. She said it was a breathing process that was having profound affects on people by providing access into unconscious memory to heal unresolved issues, even those before birth. It sounded pretty wild to me. This was long before people were exploring such ideas as "pain bodies", "cellular memory" or "mind-body connection" theories. It was unfamiliar territory, but deep inside, her message spoke to me. I felt a new sense of hope.

The very next day at breakfast, I met the President of the British Rebirthing Society. She told me more about Rebirthing and shared her own healing experiences. I sensed her inner security, a quality that still eluded me. Even though many people saw me as a free spirit, I didn't feel very free, I was so deeply hurting. When she told me about an upcoming rebirthing intensive, and said, "Oh, you can pay what you can," what did I have to lose?

In my first breathing session, I distinctly remembered being inside my mother's womb. It was hard to believe, but it was as if I could see through her belly, and was soon to be born. I remembered how much her love enveloped me. I had forgotten, since my mom and I often struggled in relationship, but this experience healed me. My longing to be with her was so deep, that I wanted to leave the workshop to find a phone. When I realized that the closest phone was too many miles away (we were in a rustic setting and this was long before cell phones), I cried, because I wanted to be "with my mommy." The memory of our deep connection filled my heart with forgiveness.

That workshop was just the beginning. Sessions, support groups and camaraderie became highlights of days that turned into weeks. My heart was emerging from an emotional prison. My British friends supported me with places to stay. My budget didn't include three extra months overseas, but God was watching over me to continue the momentum of healing.

In one session, my rebirther told me to breathe in light, like golden fire, into my lungs. My body exploded into endless space. I felt holy presence breathing me, and my heart bowed when I experienced the holiness of my own being, like a divine child coming home. My heart was so full, so open.

During my last rebirthing session in London, I lost all sense of my physical boundaries, and became part of what many have termed the Oneness. I prayed to be of deep service. It is a time I will always remember, a time when divine providence invited me onto my spiritual path.

The following story from a Bernie Siegal workshop strikes a chord deep in me: a couple arrived home with their newborn, and their three year old son anxiously awaited his brother's arrival. He insisted on being alone with him. At first, his parents were wary, fearing sibling jealousy. They resisted, but he persisted, so they finally surrendered. The mom took the precaution of turning on the baby monitor to listen. When her toddler shut the door, she heard him ask his baby brother, "Joey, can you remind me of God? I am beginning to forget."

Indeed, we all forget. The experience of birth is one of remembrance. We have the opportunity to remember the miracle of creation, love, Divine Presence - the Source of life itself. When you are truly looking into the eyes of a baby, your attention to the outer world dims and this being reflects something back to you. At times it might be the joy of witnessing gleeful gurgles and happy smiles. Sometimes, when a baby cries or is not easily consolable, it can hit up against the buried pain of your own beginning and stir inexplicable anger. The goal is self acceptance, the first step to transformation. Understanding your own beginnings truly changes how you will treat new life.

My heart's desire is to reach out to parents living in a world that is moving too fast to truly nurture the physiology of love and a spiritual life. I invite you to consider a lifelong change of focus, that is simple, yet not necessarily easy to practice. Healing is as organic as a seed planted to become a flower. Patience and trust are required. Our world needs help right now, and so do we. What I hope you will learn from reading this book is that

- Taking care of babies is sacred.

- Babies are born sweet, innocent and vulnerable.

- They deserve to be heard.

- They communicate with us, whether or not we are really paying attention.

- Babies carry the message of peace, unconditional love and compassion.

- They deserve our respect and honor.

- Babies deserve safety and protection.

- They deserve Love.

- They can bring us back to our own beginnings, to our true selves.

- Their greatest desire is to love you.

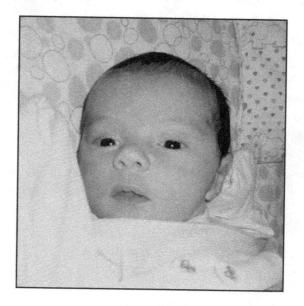

Chapter 2

The Cutting Edge in Infant Awareness Research

BRUCE LIPTON

Bruce Lipton, a world renown cellular microbiologist, has revolutionized science by discovering that our environment is equally as important as our genetic makeup, as to how we develop, what attributes are cultivated as we grow. His studies show that our individual cells have the capacity to perceive danger by constricting and moving away from a perceived threat or harmful environment. We are built with the instinct to survive *on a cellular level.*

Likewise, cells living in a nurturing environment relax and thrive. In *Biology of Belief,* Lipton says that our bodies' templates contain not just genetic information, but also information about our history.

The idea of cellular memory seemed to be abstract, until stories started to hit the media regarding heart transplant patients. The following stories show how hearts *remember.* A vegetarian received the heart of a meat eater, and started eating steaks. Even more eerie, one heart recipient was able to identify the donor's killer, because the memory was intact - it was the last person the donor saw before he died. Montel Williams featured a child on his show who had received the heart of another little girl after she died. The recipient recognized the donor's parents in the audience, although she had not met them before. Her emotion was real as she cried in their laps, reconnecting with them.

Since cellular memories are a part of our reality, it is important to examine our own belief systems. What we automatically acquire from our families or our culture isn't always life-enhancing. Some things can be damaging. Our parents never had the intention to hurt us. They probably did what their parents did. You can probably think of several things that did not contribute to high self-esteem or to feeling safe emotionally. It is not about blame, but about becoming aware. Which beliefs sustain wellness, harmony and balance? Which weigh you down or cause stress?

This is revolutionary information. When we unearth what is hidden in our unconscious, it no longer carries the same impulse, the same power. We can transform, or heal, belief systems, and replace them with a healthier reality. This so important to you as you prepare for parenthood. As babies are forming in utero, their cells are aware of their environment long before brain development. The clearer you are of negative patterning, the easier it is for your baby.

In a lecture, Bruce Lipton showed an ultrasound of a baby in utero that was taken while the parents were arguing. When they started shouting and slamming doors, the baby jumped with each forceful sound. Lipton demonstrated how a baby is affected by the adversity experienced by the parents. Even though everyone assumes that since a baby has not been born, that it is immune to outside events. Wrong. The point is that babies are an intricate part of the emotional patterns of the parents, AND are being "wired" in response to the perceived threat of the violent sounds of arguing voices.

Chapter 3

The Birth of Pre- and Perinatal Psychology

THOMAS VERNY, MD

Canadian psychiatrist Thomas Verny wrote the groundbreaking book, *The Secret Life of the Unborn Child*. His pioneer research gave birth to the field of prenatal and perinatal psychology. He founded the Association of Pre- & Perinatal Psychology and Health (APPPAH), to increase the awareness of how conception, pregnancy and birth have lifelong impact on babies, families, and societies. The website is www.birthpsychology.com

I met Thomas Verny during his book tour, shortly after my return to the US. It was a relief to find someone who not only related to my recent healing experiences, but also validated them. He inspired me. His book describes how life in our mother's womb has a deep dimension of consciousness that scientists are only beginning to understand.

Verny spoke of how mothers transmit messages that could shape the baby's self image, even in the womb. This effect was not so much about fleeting thoughts, worries, doubts or fears. It was more about deep, persistent feelings, such as chronic anxiety, wrenching ambivalence about motherhood, or downright rejection, all of which could deeply scar an unborn child emotionally. He spoke of the lifelong templates that are created during pregnancy. The most significant influence on the psyche of the baby was the emotional state of the mother. The second most significant was how the baby's dad felt towards the mom.[1]

Verny discovered that the majority of his psychotherapy clients had highly charged prenatal histories and/or some kind of birth trauma. They also reported a lot of pain during the birthing process and were very aware of their own mother's stress.[2]

One story he recounted came from a German hypnotherapist, whose male client had suffered anxiety attacks associated with hot flashes. With hypnosis, the client remembered a crucial prenatal experience. As the therapist guided him into the seventh month of his gestation, the client began to feel panic and fear. He recalled that his mother had attempted to abort him by taking extremely hot baths. (She later verified this.) He hadn't understood the source of the danger, but it was imbedded in his memory. Once the light was shed into this dark space, he was able to understand, forgive, and heal.[3]

On the lighter side, Verny related a story of a cellist from Ontario Philharmonic, whose mother, also a cellist, played certain pieces of music while she was pregnant with him. He never had to learn those particular pieces. He just knew them "by heart."

One Verny study confirmed how much prenatal smoking stresses the unborn child. He noted that even the mother's thinking of smoking created a stress response in the baby: increased movement, increased heart rate, as if to anticipate the inevitable rapid decrease of oxygen that results from the effects of nicotine.[4]

After years of research, Verny concluded that "intrauterine bonding" did not happen automatically. Love for the child and understanding of one's own feelings were essential components that could more than offset the ordinary emotional disturbances of daily life.[5]

No one is immune to adversity. No matter how hard a woman tries to have a peaceful pregnancy, something can happen. As a result, the baby is flooded with maternal hormones in reaction to a shocking event. But it is only damaging if a mother is so distracted by her loss that she withdraws from her baby for an extended period of time. If she manages to keep herself in connection with her baby with reassuring messages, then they both continue to thrive, this prevents long-term emotional pain.[6]

The stories in Verny's book highlight the consciousness we carry as babies. So much would change if healing attention were given during the entire process of creating a tiny life. It certainly would offset the pain and constriction that happens with stressful circumstances. This information emphasizes how crucial connection is. When a mom communicates and creates meaning with her baby, she sets up a template of love and safety that cushions her baby from the inevitable stressors in life.

After reading Verny's book, along with my own healing experiences, I had the perfect environment to put it to good use. It had been years since I worked as a nurse. The familiar hospital environment felt so strange now, because my own being and perception had changed. On my first day back to work, I stood in the doorway of the NICU, transfixed by the scene. All the babies, premature and/or in physical distress, were surrounded by medical personnel, stressed themselves as they cared for these babies. It was a very busy and intense atmosphere.

All I could focus on were the babies! Sentient beings, fully aware, recording memories, with no understanding of their environment. No one really knew who these infants were and what they were perceiving and feeling. I remembered my prayer to be of deep service. Here it was, right in front of me.

I was shy and introverted about my new frontier, and I was new at this hospital. I worried that people would think I was crazy. That didn't stop me from holding my babies with a deeper awareness, or from knowing how important it was to talk to them. I started out by telling them why they were in the hospital, where their parents were, how much their parents missed them. If no one was telling them, how would they know?

One baby in the unit was eight months old. He was born extremely premature. His recovery and development was a long road home. His name was Caesar, and he truly was the king of the NICU. Everyone loved Caesar; after all, they had all nursed him to health. They loved his great personality. The nurses visited frequently, even when he wasn't their patient. The time had come for him to be discharged. In his case, his physical care was involved. Teaching time was complicated by limited visiting hours, plus a scared teenage mom. When the nurses found out he was finally going home, they told him how much they would miss him.

Discharge day arrived, but Caesar developed a fever, so going home was postponed. They didn't find any source of infection. They rescheduled. The night before he was next scheduled to go home, he threw up and choked on his milk. Again, a delay, since he had history of pneumonia. I met his mother briefly. She was timid, frightened, and handled Caesar like a stranger, which was understandable, considering the circumstances. As this scenario unfolded, it was really clear to me what was happening. I waited for an opportune moment to spend some time alone with Caesar.

I told him that I knew exactly what was going on: he was afraid of going home. It made sense! He was used to his many familiar caregivers, not the one scared person who was his mother. I explained to him that his mother's love was much greater than the love of any number of nurses, and that up until now, he was living in the ugliest room in the world. I described flowers and rainbows and ice cream and friends and family. I ended with: "If you don't like it out there, you can always come back."

It was amazing how intent he was on listening to me, how prolonged his gaze was. Usually he looked around and didn't focus much. I like to think that he got the message, because he went home the next day. He did come back a month later, but since he had been "out" in the world, he was admitted to a different unit. He had an immediate recovery. My guess is that it wasn't the family reunion with his nurses that he had expected, and he wanted to leave as soon as possible.

I found this scenario exciting. It really worked to talk to him. It encouraged me to keep communicating, explaining to the babies. I wanted to keep filling in the blanks, to give them the information they needed so that they would not feel helpless and afraid. I wanted to fill them with hope.

What does this mean for you as parents? The idea that cells have memory makes you realize how important it is for a mom to take care of herself. Cortisol, the stress hormone, constricts babies in many ways, especially since their cells are multiplying so rapidly. Too much cortisol sends a message to the baby's cells that life is not safe. The cells think they are in danger, and go into survival mode, rather than into nurturance mode.

The reason most moms run themselves ragged during their pregnancies is because their own mothers did, as did their grandmothers. Our ancestors were instrumental in creating our initial patterning, and these habits are generations old. This is **not** about creating guilt, it is about change. Understanding the consequences of your actions and making appropriate changes is the ultimate preventive medicine. As a pregnant woman, your self care *helps your baby. It also erases the history of your lineage.* This is the ultimate healing, to erase harmful patterns and not pass them onto your baby.

Now is the time to make that commitment. What is one small thing you can do for yourself **every day**, that will nurture your body, your heart and your soul?

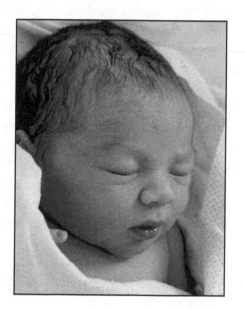

Chapter 4

From the Baby's Point of View

David Chamberlain, PhD

Psychologist David Chamberlain worked with Verny to promote the revolutionary understanding of babies' level of awareness. A past president of APPPAH, he wrote *The Mind of Your Newborn Baby*, which is available in twelve languages. It is an extremely valuable resource for parents to read at any time, but especially before they conceive a child. It offers insight into what birth is like from the baby's point of view.

Freud entertained the idea that adverse birth memories were stored in the unconscious, creating fear and anxiety. He surmised that birth trauma could be the origin of lifelong upheaval.[7]

Chamberlain also studied birth memory, proving that it was real and not fantasy. In his literature, he cited the use of breath work (similar to the rebirthing breathing process that proved to be so healing for me). Around 1980, psychiatrist Stanislav Grof used a similar breathing process to help clients uncover events that led to negative patterns. Grof's findings showed common themes emerging from similar birth circumstances. For example:

- Unwanted pregnancies produce children who expect rejection.
- Children born by Caesarian section have a hard time completing things on their own.
- Incubator babies feel separated from the world, and from love. The glass wall isolated them from the rest of the world.[8]

These findings validated my own experiences. I had attended several rebirthing workshops in Holland. During the workshops, many participants remembered horror stories of being born during World War II. Some recalled the bombing and starvation that permeated their lives as babies. With the insights they gained in their sessions, they understood the lifelong anxiety of not feeling safe. By bringing the Spirit of the breath into the memory of their past, they broke free of pain. Using their breath in a conscious manner, they brought light into buried events that had created the dark fears and defense systems in the first place.

One man from Amsterdam lamented that he had not been very successful in creating relationships. He lived like a hermit. In a series of sessions he remembered being in an incubator, feeling abandoned. He saw himself lying "in a box, alone" for great lengths of time. He realized how fearful he was. If someone approached him, it often led to pain, be it from a heel stick for blood, or starting an IV, or being suctioned. The most painful aspect of his flashbacks was how little anyone had spoken to him during these procedures.

What impressed me about this man was how stiff his posture was at the first workshop. His demeanor was guarded. His armor, both physical and emotional, had been his survival. He was protecting that vulnerable infant who had endured so many struggles alone. Remarkably, after using breath therapy, his whole being relaxed. He brought closure to his rough beginnings. Discovering his birth memories gave him a new perspective. After living his whole adult life alone, he married within the year.

Another remarkable case was Margo, a young girl in her twenties, who complained of nagging depression and feelings of grief, yet had no explanation for it. Through Rebirthing, she remembered having a twin sister who was stillborn. After the workshop, she went home to ask her mom if this was true. Her mother admitted that she had withheld that information to "protect" her surviving daughter, thinking that knowing about the stillbirth would upset her.

In Margo's next session, she intentionally went back to the time when she enjoyed a deep bond with her twin who kept her company in utero. Eventually she recalled lying next to her sister's lifeless body toward the end of the pregnancy. She remembered feeling helpless, wondering what had happened. She shed tears of grief. She was then able to say goodbye to her sister, to lay the memory to rest. She also forgave those who never spoke of her twin.

This story shows that secrecy is felt and produces feelings of isolation, especially for the person from whom the truth is withheld. No matter how bad it may seem, no matter how good the intention, it creates separation and confusion for even the smallest of creatures. Since babies are exquisitely sensitive, they can be very aware of those "elephants in the room".

In Chamberlain's ground-breaking work, he used hypnosis to invite birth memories. It was a profound way to discover the deep feelings that babies actually experience. Through this method of recall, he documented how extensively we carry our past. He coined the phrase "psychological birthmarks" to describe pivotal events that create wounding. *Painful memories remain elusive until their origin is revealed.*[9]

Before the study, Chamberlain interviewed couplets of mothers and their grown children. The initial criterion was that none of his subjects had previously recalled or discussed the birth experience with each other. The moms ranged from 32-46 years old; the children 9-23 years old. In hypnosis he let them tell their stories. The sessions were recorded, transcribed and compared. Neither parent nor child were present at each other's hypnosis session. Each spoke freely as the memories came to the surface.[10]

The recall of the birth event was accurate and the mother/child stories matched. Each child's details showed uncanny awareness in describing the birth story. The children revealed frequent themes:

- They expressed common feelings and concerns.
- They described labor while they were inside the womb.
- Their details of labor and delivery were verified by parents and other observers.
- They wondered where their dad was if the father was absent.
- They clearly knew their mothers' initial reactions to seeing them.
- They knew when they were the "wrong" gender.
- They appreciated gentle handling and/or protested when it was rough.
- They wanted immediate contact with mom after delivery.
- They lamented separation from mom, and felt abandoned when left alone.
- They felt like objects when there was no communication with handling.
- They were surprised when people talked about them, but not to them.[11]

I knew all too well how damaging comments and reactions could be. My frequent rebirthing sessions unearthed clues, subtle impressions and clear memories on a regular basis. My family of origin always struggled with tension, illness, lack of money, and my father's own bouts of depression and post-traumatic stress from World War II. I was born by default, more like "the fault" of rhythm method birth control. By delving into my own prenatal memories, I experienced my mother's dread and fear. Her psychology became mine. It became clear to me that her anxiety had very much to do with another pregnancy that they could not afford. When I asked my mom about it, she admitted that she did not want to be pregnant again. She assured me that it was not about me, but more about the heavy circumstances. She responded truthfully and filled in the blanks for me. I came to understand why I felt like such a burden to everyone, and felt responsible for everyone's pain.

Another pivotal memory surfaced during a deep-massage session. Relaxed yet attentive to my body, I was breathing to allow knotted muscles to release. As the therapist worked on my left wrist, I *heard* an old thought: *I wasn't okay the way I was, so they had to cut something out of me.* I was stunned. When I was five years old, I had surgery to remove a mole from my left wrist, a mole that was large, hairy and ugly. This memory was significant, it seemed. In my next rebirthing session, I discovered what was behind that thought. As the session progressed, I felt confused and angry. I then remembered how much time people spent talking about this mole when I was born. I couldn't believe it! Every time someone would meet me (as a baby), they would comment how cute I was... but then oh, too bad *there was something wrong with her.* I wanted them to know that I was perfect the way I was. That was how God created me. I kept hearing that I was flawed. I realized how negatively I had been affected by these frequent thoughtless comments.

My heart grieved for not being celebrated for who I was, the way I was. I wanted to be received in my own unique beauty, in my own perfection. I wanted everyone to be happy with me as I was. I longed for that acceptance.

I left this session feeling very raw, vulnerable and sad. Later that night, something happened to help me see this as a blessing. I was at work, and one of my patients was suffering many complications. His surgical wound was infected, tender and swollen. He was sick and obviously in pain. He was in my arms and I was feeding him. An intern approached. Without any introduction or explanation, he pressed on the baby's head, on his tender incision. The baby cried in pain. The intern, oblivious to the cry, muttered, "This baby is a mess." He left as quickly as he came. My eyes welled with tears as I comfort this little guy. "You know, sweetie, I want to apologize for him. He just doesn't know who you are. I had someone talk about me that way when I was your age, and I know how much it hurts. It hurts a lot. But you know what? Even though you have something wrong with you right now, it doesn't mean that you will have something wrong with you for the rest of your life. You can heal. Trust me, you will be okay. The angels are with you. God is with you. And your mom and dad really love you. I am so sorry that this happened to you. He didn't know any better."

How attentive he was to my heartfelt words! I knew he was connecting on some level. I realized how much I have in common with these delicate infants. What a blessing! I knew from my own experience how important it was to see babies from their point of view, to recognize them, accept them, and give them respect. And again, to give them HOPE.

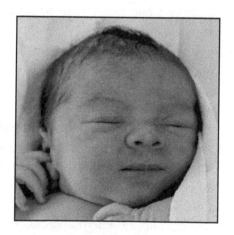

Chapter 5

The Evidence of Patterns

Wendy Anne McCarty, PhD

Dr. Wendy Anne McCarty has been integral in the development of the academic program of Prenatal and Perinatal Psychology at the Santa Barbara Graduate Institute. McCarty's research sheds light into the mysteries of early life, including even before conception.

With her colleague Ray Castellino, a chiropractic doctor and healer, she established a research clinic which provided innovative, gentle interventions with young babies and their parents to resolve early stress. The therapists videotaped sessions to closely examine what and how infants were communicating. Parents came seeking assistance with bonding issues or adverse behaviors that they noted in their babies, not knowing that emotional trauma was involved. The researchers' observations were based on the assumption that all of us, from infancy, demonstrate and repeat patterns that reflect painful events or circumstances that need to be healed. No matter how young, babies sense when something isn't right. They also call for clarity, comfort, safety and the truth, in their own way.

McCarty suggests that prenatal and perinatal memory and traumatic imprints are expressed by the babies in patterns. They always want to communicate with us, to share their stories, their impressions. That is their nature. Our nature! She related that as she and Castellino observed babies, they discovered patterns of distress that could be traced back to stressful or traumatic experiences -- prenatally, at birth, or both.

In *The Power of Beliefs*, McCarty proposed that prenatal and birth experiences lay the foundation of subconscious beliefs and life patterns. These beliefs influence how we see and feel about ourselves and our world. They are reflected in all levels of our being from our earliest memories, as well as from our parents. [12]

This holds relevance for parents to understand how important it is to heal their own unresolved issues. The baby is then free to develop more life-enhancing beliefs.[13] This is the greatest gift parents can give, to open the doorway for their babies to develop naturally and express their authentic selves in love and in safety.

The therapists studied the videos of the therapy sessions to detect the hidden messages in their client-babies' actions. What were the babies communicating? Through observation and interview, they often identified forgotten memories or factors that created stress during conception, pregnancy and/or the birthing process. Once the parents confirmed a *missing piece*, they were able to address it with their baby. The baby's behavior would then change, sometimes slowly, sometimes more dramatically. The end result was that the babies bonded with their parents more easily. The problems were resolved.

In one case, the parents' concern was that when their baby tried to stand up and walk, she would not put her feet together. Instead, she adopted a split-leg posture, which made it impossible for her to move in balance. After many questions, it still was not clear. McCarty's intuition prompted her to ask if anything out of the ordinary had happened to the mom when she was the same age as her daughter. The mother recalled a memory so deeply buried that she had not realized the significance it still held. She had been born with dislocated hips and was put in a spica cast with a stabilizing bar. The cast kept her legs in a wide-split position for three months. McCarty asked if she had ever had any healing or therapy around clearing this traumatic experience. Mom admitted that she had not. The piece of the puzzle came to light. The baby was replicating the posture of her mother with a cast. In a following session, the mother went gently into a silent inner process, connecting with her inner infant, empathizing with all that she had experienced during this ordeal. The mother emerged saying that she had felt a healing by acknowledging the past. The baby awoke and moved from her father's arms to her mother's side. The next time the baby attempted to stand, she put her feet together for the first time. McCarty suggested that the mother's unresolved issue carried over and that the baby had identified with it. As the mother addressed and healed some aspect of her traumatic early experience, that trauma was released by her child as well.

The impact of mom's healing was that her baby never displayed the same posture again. It is remarkable to me that babies resonate with their parents so completely that they adopt their patterns, carrying them on as a part of their identity, even though the pattern itself is not originally their own.

The major implication in this research is how crucial it is to see life from the babies' point of view, *and how much we can glean from them if we listen.* The tiniest of babies yearn to be heard. Think of times when you needed to be heard, and were ignored, cut off, or ridiculed. When we are heard with a deep heart and in sincerity, healing can occur. When we are held in integrity, we can more easily stay connected to the Divine. We learn that we are safe. Truth, respect and love become the primary ingredients in relationship.

So what happens when we are not heard? Were you seen and not heard as a child?

According to my parents, I cried constantly for my first three months. I already knew that I was not a planned or welcomed addition. I was also vulnerable to the wild and crazy world at home. After attending McCarty's workshop, I booked a private healing session with her. I was excited about the possibilities of what I would learn.

Filling out her preparation form took over three hours. As I described my parents as individuals, more memories emerged. The writing exercise alone made me ripe for the session. The depth of the anxiety and worry that I re-experienced in utero during the regression was very heavy, yet transformative, as I took another step deeper into the truth.

McCarty's insight was validating and helpful. She put context to my experience: "You had no choice but to swim in your mother's despair about having no money. *And* the violence and anger around her. You bore it just like she did, the whole time you were inside. When you cried as an infant, you were trying to let them know that something was wrong (about how much fighting was going on). They could not understand you, nor your message. You reminded them of their own pain, which was already too much for them." My perspective of my family grew more compassionate.

Her feedback reframed my memory. She reminded me that that was then and this is now. The memory is there, but I need not fall victim to my history. She demonstrated a deep respect by hearing and acknowledging my message. My heart had been heard.

Chapter 6

The Remembrance

The preceding chapters have been filled with information about how important it is to nurture your unborn child, yet it is hard to give if you feel depleted. You can have a lot of material goods in your life, but yet not be content. Burnout lurks when outer demands never stop and your inner well dries up. Do you resent work, go home feeling empty, yet you have a family that needs you? Are you reaching a crossroads? When you feel like something is missing in your life, your heart is calling you to change, to give up what isn't working for you. When you have feelings like this, it is time to redefine yourself. When you yearn for something new, something to feed your heart, you open the door for transformation. This is especially important if you are planning to have children, or if you already have them.

Connecting to your baby before birth is the most important thing you can do, along with taking care of yourself. To prepare, you must lay the groundwork to be connected to *yourself*, a great challenge in our fast-paced world. There is a simple way for you to bring it all together through the practice of Remembrance. It is a way of connecting throughout the day to the Living Presence within your heart, the Source of life itself. It helps you to *remember, as babies do, who you really are.*

This practice is not a one time thing. Filling up with the Divine every day should be a priority, especially when you are bringing new life into the world. It is what your soul desires, to acknowledge and cherish yourself as a container of creation. Divine Presence is our only Constant in this life. It is important to stay tethered, especially with all the turbulence in the world.

The Remembrance is a prayer practice that will prepare you for Divine Parenthood, and create a lifelong bond for you with your baby. It will give you and your baby spiritual medicine at the same time. Your practice can help you feel the certainty of Love within. You will be amazed by how simple yet profound that can be.

Years ago, I met a medical doctor who was committed to spiritual transformation in health care. He taught the ancient prayer tradition of the Remembrance: repeating the name of God into the heart while sitting in silence, focusing on the heart to create a holy, expansive space. It deepened my awareness of my inner refuge. The more I focused, the easier it became. I became quieter, less overwhelmed by personal affairs or outside circumstances. I discovered an intimate relationship with the Presence. It has been a profound, life-changing process. My health improved, my heart is thriving, and I am eternally grateful for the deepening connection.

It's too easy to lose yourself when you are stressed by too many demands. When you forget who you really are - a *spiritual being* - you feel the pain of separation. The remedy is to remember the Presence within your heart. Whether you are Christian, Jew, Muslim, Hindu, Buddhist - or any religion - you carry It. When you know the true essence of your religion, you see only Love.

This practice can help you be the kind of person and parent you want to be: the parent your baby needs. It helps you to keep your family intact. Anyone, everyone, can find peace and harmony within. Again, it is not a quick fix. It takes time and practice, but the reward is a rich and everlasting context to help you live your life in Love.

Getting Started

Intention is important. It plants the seed of change. Usually we focus on what we want to get rid of, rather than what we want to create. First, feel your deep desire to be held in Love. If you carry many burdens in your life, this practice gives you the opportunity to put them down. This quiet time with your Source will help you to remember that you are not alone.

Before you begin, find or create a quiet space for yourself. Shut off your TV, cell phone, music, everything! If you are used to activity, noise, and people, being alone and quiet can feel strange, even unsettling. Eventually, though, the silence will feed your heart and soul.

Sit comfortably. Put your hand over your heart to bring your attention there. Feel the rise and fall of your chest while you breathe. Be aware of yourself sitting in the chair, your feet on the floor. Notice any tension in your body. Allow yourself to relax. Now imagine that you can breathe directly in and out of your heart, right through your chest wall. Start repeating your name for God. Use the word or name that makes your heart feel reverent. Examples of "The Name" are *Lord, Beloved Lord, Yahweh, Jesus, Christus, Allah, Krishna, Om.* Or you may simply repeat *Love* or *The One*.

Continue to repeat The Name, quietly, softly.

What is happening in your heart? It may be difficult to notice at first, especially if you are not used to being still. It may sound strange, but your heart has more neural cells than your brain, so it does think and feel. With practice, you will trust what your heart is feeling. As you practice, you may feel your heart expand, feel deeper reverence. As you do this, it opens you more deeply to the divine. It helps you to embrace your challenges and become more empowered within yourself, connecting to yourself, to the Presence.

Your mind will probably wander. This is normal. The mind is always busy in thought. Trying to fight it is a distraction of its own. Imagine it as being a distant noise, but your attention is elsewhere. For example, you can be engrossed in a TV program, but your most favorite person calls. When you are on the phone, the volume of the TV has not changed. You can still hear it, but your focus is on your friend. Treat your thoughts like the TV, and return ever so gently to the Name. This allows you to relax into the practice more:

Slowly, receive the Presence.

Repeat the Name to recognize the love within.

When you are in the state of remembering, eventually your focus will change:

You will feel love.

You will feel safer.

You will remember more easily that you are not alone.

Continue the practice, even if nothing seems to be happening. Change is often a process, slow and subtle. Just like your baby, growth is necessary before transformation takes place. *Remember*, you are worth it.

Can it be that simple? How often do you suffer from obsessive thinking, without asking for help or spiritual support? Eckhart Tolle, in *A New Earth*, warned that we have reached a time where we must evolve or die. We are all searching for solutions during this complex period in human history. It would be of utmost value to include the Remembrance in your life. Before seeking outside advice, go within and ask for help. Then, and only then, start to act. You will more likely recognize right action when you are not overwhelmed by stress.

The Remembrance develops a deeper reliance on the Presence that sustains you. Many people call this Presence God. Some call upon the One, a Higher Power, or Love. The more you focus on the Living One inside you, the more holy and loving your life becomes. It is a solid way to access the stillness within. The more anchored you are in the Love, the less validation you need from the outside world.

As your heart connection gets deeper, you are more able to be a holy container for your baby, transmitting love and safety in a natural way that empowers you to be the spiritual anchor of your family.

On a practical level, there are many benefits to the Remembrance. When your heart is full, it is easier to be compassionate. You can forgive yourself for your shortcomings, which makes it much easier to forgive others. You will dramatically reduce the stress in your life, thereby increasing the health and intelligence of your unborn baby. And you will be encoding your baby with Remembering who he/she really is, just like the musician mom did by playing music for her unborn baby.

That is how amazingly powerful your love is. You can give yourself the greatest gift by remembering who you are, empowering yourself for parenthood. Knowing how you feel is crucial to your well being. When you are aware of your present state, you can more easily identify what *you* need in the moment. Yes, your attention is focused on yourself, rather than on others. It may seem selfish to think of yourself first, but self awareness brings you clarity over time. You can then be that person who gives from an authentic space, from the Well that never runs dry.

The Remembrance can be a lifesaver for you, when you are trying to meet the constant needs of your baby, your family, your work. When you feel stressed and powerless you are probably trying to manage life all alone, and usually blaming yourself for your shortcomings. When you feel this way, come back to yourself. Forgive yourself for being human. Remember to go inside to your sanctuary. Ask for help *first, from your Divine Source, especially when everything seems to be falling apart.*

Like any relationship, inner connection takes time. The more you practice, the better it gets. You become more and more aware of the Living Presence in your heart, in your life. The more you remember, the deeper your heart focus.

You can surrender in a new way. When you feel sad or angry, bring it to heart. There is a therapeutic space that exists between ignoring pain and indulging in it. Allow yourself to feel your pain, and bring the Name into that feeling. This can transform a painful state. The change may not be "in the blink of an eye," but it will come. You will gain an understanding of yourself that is far beyond the limits of your personality or your ego. This is the secret. You cannot give what you do not have. It is only by giving yourself mercy that you can be merciful.

Your job is to fill up first.

This is the greatest gift that you can give yourself, your family, your community. By seeing yourself as a child of God, you do the same for others. When you are anchored in love, everything you do and say is healing. When you are not, you have the opportunity to forgive yourself for being human, and be humble enough to ask within, what you need to learn from this. It is the deepest way to heal yourself: by connecting to your divinity and seeing that divinity in others. The ripple effect is huge. If you want to help create a better world, do this.

Chapter 7

Remembering During Pregnancy

Prenatal Bonding

Wendy McCarty's research illustrated the intrinsic connection between mother and baby. In the example of the little girl whose mom had worn a spica cast, the baby demonstrated the memory, even though it belonged to the mom. Fortunately, the baby's message was heard. The mother had closure to heal her own pain, and the baby dropped the story as well.

The Remembrance can help you to clear old emotional issues. Being consistent with your practice, present in love, is the ultimate preparation and gift for future generations. As you heal unresolved issues, your baby can naturally evolve and express authentic love and safety. If you start now, It also prepares you to conceive in love. Your baby will be nurtured by your growing spiritual awareness.

Many moms-to-be find the Remembrance invaluable as they transition into motherhood. Since pregnancy is a time of change, the more time you devote to preparing, the more you can soften the inevitable stressors in life. When you connect to a loving, peaceful, intentional state, you can transmit that love and safety to the baby, and you both benefit greatly.

Research done in the twentieth century by Dr. Jeno Raffai included work with 1200 pregnant women in Hungary during a twenty-year period. He used his own method of the bonding process. The moms were guided within, allowing themselves images, feelings, communication from their babies. Dr. Gerald Schroth from Germany introduced the Bonding

Analysis method (created by Raffai) to the United States to deepen and enrich the birthing process here.

The moms in Raffai's study developed a deep intuitive sense during their bonding sessions. They became aware of how their babies were developing, and some even sensed impending complications as they developed. This allowed early intervention with impressive results:

- Mother and baby were a team during labor and delivery, with less fear and pain.
- The incidence of birth trauma was markedly decreased compared to the rate noted from "normal" hospital births.
- There was less need for anesthetics, and episiotomies were rare.
- There was not one case of postpartum depression.
- There were only two premature births. (The average rate is 15%.)
- Over time, awareness between mom and baby created higher self-esteem for both.

These results support the idea that connection is the key. Through the Bonding Analysis process, the babies felt seen and heard in utero. That there was no postpartum depression shows how beneficial the process was for the moms as well. You can see how effective Bonding Analysis was for all the women in the study. Adding a spiritual focus using the Remembrance can further enhance the prenatal bonding process. It prepares you to be the heart of your family.

As you do the Remembrance while pregnant, allow your heart to feel expanded, *enveloping* your womb. Enfold your baby in divine reality by breathing in the Name. This is the language your baby truly understands, the language of Love. This aspect of Remembrance is called **holding your baby's heart.** You are not **sending love, you are being love.** Sending implies that your baby is a distance away, but this is not true. Your **beings** are unified, one and the same.

Prenatal bonding and holding your baby's heart give you the space to fall in Love with your baby. Invite your baby to communicate with you. You now know how sentient and aware babies are. Your baby so wants to connect to you, to love you, to be received. What a gift!

As you sit in the stillness, your intuition deepens. If you are kinesthetic, you probably *feel* things. Perhaps in your imagination, you see, and more easily *visualize*. Or maybe you have a sense of *knowing*. However you perceive, you can develop a sense of who your baby is before birth by just taking the time.

In this way, you also prepare your baby for the birthing process. You are a team, rather than being passive and having birth done to you. This was how Dr. Raffai performed his deliveries. His moms *knew* if their babies developed stress, and acted accordingly. They were *empowered* by the birthing process, and became *empowered* mothers of babies who grew up confident and secure, because they were *held* as an integral part of the team, rather than as the object of a medical procedure.

For Example

Practicing the Remembrance during pregnancy really helped Lilly. She was two months pregnant, frantic about past miscarriages, and worried that she would have another one. By relying on the Name, she faced her fears. As she practiced, she developed trust as she experienced being held in the arms of the Divine. Her heart focus provided peace and refuge. From that space, she learned to hold her baby's heart, rather than transmitting worry and fear. Her grief resolved. She felt more present, able to provide emotional safety to her baby. She invited her baby to *stay*. With their connection, she began to relax and actually enjoy her pregnancy.

As you prepare, use these steps to, plant the seeds for an enriched family life:

Create a baby altar to honor your baby's life.

Take care of yourself.

Be accepting of who you are and of your own nature.

Take time for yourself. Be still.

Go inside, into your sanctuary where you can drink from the Source.

Then it will easier to be with your children.

To hold their hearts.

To cherish them.

To experience their joy.

And, as time goes on,

To keep them remembering as well

    That they are the Love.

    That they are children of the Divine

    That they are hidden treasures yearning to be known.

As you prepare for the birth, please do your research. People often learn more about the cars they buy, than about how they are going to deliver. It is up to you to create the best start for your family. The truth within you is the ultimate authority. Go inside, look for solutions, trust your guidance, trust yourself. No matter what happens, whether it goes as planned or not, don't forget to Remember.

Chapter 8

Transformation Into Motherhood

So how do you keep it all together, when there is a lot of uncertainty about the future? Especially if your life is stressed, it is inevitable that someone will annoy you or make you angry. That is human nature. When your feelings get hurt, the end result is negative feelings towards someone. You don't realize how deeply you can affect others with thoughts and feelings, both positive and negative. Yet there is scientific evidence that proves that to be true.

Dr. Masuru Emoto, a Japanese microbiologist, discovered that water responds to human emotion. He examined numerous samples of water from various sources under the microscope. Water from glaciers appeared to possess a magnificent, beautiful crystalline structure. Water from a sewage system, on the other hand, had a murky distorted structure.

Emoto put water from the same source into various flasks. Different words were printed on the flasks, such as *love, appreciation, gratitude, hate, you fool,* and *anger.* The flasks labeled with positive words developed exquisite crystalline structures. The others developed distorted structures similar to the sewer water. He then took the flasks labeled with negative words, relabeled them with the word *love, and the structure transformed into clear crystal.*[14]

In another experiment, Emoto gave water to children to hold, and after a short time, the crystalline structure of the water changed dramatically as shown in before and after pictures. It became more beautiful: more evidence that babies and children can be medicine for parents! A display of Emoto's photography on You Tube shows much more about his experiments. It is crucial to understand the power of words and feelings, especially in regard to infants.

Babies' bodies in utero are ninety-nine percent water.[15] This explains how important it is for them to be loved and appreciated. The same goes for adults, who are about eighty percent water. Imagine how beautiful is the crystalline structure of the water in your and your children's bodies when you are connecting to their hearts! Practicing the Remembrance greatly influences your health, your baby's health, and anyone else whom you hold in deep love and respect. You have the chance to create a crystal-clear baby!

Bonding is simpler before birth than it is once children are older, but at any age, it works. I heard this story in one of the many classes I have attended over the years. It illustrates how effective and dramatic it can be for you to change your perspective, your relationship, no matter how challenging. It shows how strongly we affect our environment and the people in it.

An inner city school had declined due to violence, drugs, teen pregnancy and a high dropout rate. The faculty feared for their own lives, and their classes were chaos. They became so frustrated that they sought outside help. The teachers were taught to connect to the hearts of their students. They learned to become still within themselves before class started. Then they held the class roster, visualizing each student, name by name, connecting heart to heart. Eventually, they were able to do this *during* class. Within six months, the student body was transformed. The students started to study and get involved. They admitted that they felt more respected, and were inspired to reach their potential. ***Their hearts were being held.*** All this was done without invoking the Divine. Imagine the effect you can have on anyone, even a perfect stranger, let alone your own children, by intention, in the name of Love.

Transforming Yourself

How wonderful it would be if the outside world would become perfect so that finding peace would be easy. As much as you would like that to happen, the change can only start with you. You cannot change the fact that you experience negativity. Again, that is a part of being human, but it is not a place where you want to live. Over time through this practice, you can transform your point of view. Harboring resentment and judgment hurts your own heart, and that it just is not worth the consequences.

During pregnancy, your moods change, you feel vulnerable and scared at times. This can make relationships really tricky. When you find yourself feeling sad, alone, disconnected from your life, your partner, try to Remember. Allow your feelings to surface. Do not be afraid of them. When you bring them into the light, they lose power. As you bring your feelings *to heart*, breathe the Name into them. Ask for help. Stay with it until you feel at least neutral, or even better, more connected to yourself. It will help you gain perspective. Sometimes needing to be right can work against you. Remember that others also experience their own fears or feelings of separation. When you see that both sides are in pain and wanting love, you can be forgiving of yourself. Then you can more easily forgive others. We all need Love. Your choice to love your partner despite fear and conflict helps to create a healthier bond, and it will transform the situation by each seeing the other as innocent. You can hold someone else's heart much more easily when you feel that the Divine is holding yours. Again, this inner refuge is your only constant, for life and relationships are always changing. Always!

Clearing old wounds is essential to be parenting with a deep heart. A baby's cry, especially an inconsolable one, can trigger old patterns of pain. When you push away emotions, feeling guilty that you want your baby to stop crying or else, STOP. Accept that you have reached your limit. Give yourself the space to notice your thoughts and feelings. Do you want to start screaming? Do you think that feeling frustrated makes you a bad mom? Do you want to run away? Take those feelings to heart and go into Remembrance. Once you embrace a reaction with love and forgiveness, it starts to fade. It may return, but with less power and a clearer perspective. Your compassionate awareness diffuses it. Humbly, wisely, accept your humanity and ask God for help. There will be times that your baby will test your patience, possibly all through life. Ask for inner help first, then for outer help when you need it. Take care of your own needs first. It takes a brief moment! *Put on the oxygen mask - the Divine - first, then take care of others.* Once you take care of yourself, your heart, you are able to accept your own limits. Once you are clear, you can hold your baby, be a comfort for his/her pain with love, without being triggered yourself. This process is an essential ingredient for heart-filled parenting.

For Example

Susan found this practice extremely helpful to relieve marital tension. Her husband's depression intensified during her pregnancy. She became angry about his lack of support was spinning emotionally, totally obsessed by his lack of attention. By learning the Remembrance, she became less reactive, more accepting. She practiced holding her baby's heart, letting her baby know that she was welcomed, that she was safe, and that her mom's stress had nothing to do with her. Susan found that the more she was able to be in her heart, the less stress she felt. She sat in Remembrance, seeing the Divine in her husband. She gradually became more patient with his state, and the more she held his heart, the more he responded to her. Susan realized that she had been looking for help and solutions outside herself. She had convinced herself that she could not count on her husband, and had even lined up other people to help her during the birth. In her Remembrance practice, she started to ask God for help first, and things always worked out, not necessarily in the way she thought, but often better than she had anticipated. She continues the practice of holding the hearts of her family. She finds it helps her to create a far better, calmer atmosphere at home.

Remember every day:

Get excited about your transformation.

Love and appreciate who you are and who you are becoming.

There is a Divine Mother living within you to hold your heart.

Allow yourself to be held.

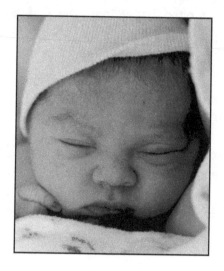

Chapter 9

Parenting from the Deep Heart

Parenting in these complex, troubled times is not an easy task. Trying to control and manage all of your responsibilities and concerns can be overwhelming. Now you know a beautiful way to increase your reliance on the Deep Love. On a core level, you are the barometer of your child's sense of safety from the time of conception. When moms relax, babies relax. Their beings, their cells thrive. They feel safe and respected.

Research in Scandinavia revealed that 98% of the prison inmates had a history of birth trauma and/or prolonged separation from their mothers. Babies who experience adversity don't automatically grow up to be criminals, but the chances of long-term consequences do increase with trauma and prolonged separation.

Attachment disorders can develop when babies do not have the chance to truly, deeply bond with their mothers. The biochemistry in the brain necessary to create trusting relationships can be impaired. The bonding process is an ongoing connection which takes years. It is a part of nature. Connection, relationship takes time and cultivation. Speed of life weakens the process. When life moves so fast that mother and baby do not spend extended quality time together, attachment can still happen, but sometimes not deeply enough. If this is not recognized and addressed, children can grow up with a "blind spot" about relationships, and not understand how their actions affect other people. Perhaps this is why there has been a dramatic rise in violence in our school-age children.

Children-turned-criminals don't come from "bad families." Births have become too mechanical, too fast, and the physiology of love itself is altered in the process. This is further complicated by the fact that precious family time together has dramatically decreased in our society. This is a grave issue, and now you have a way to nurture your connection!

When you worry about someone in your family, use the Remembrance to *hold the heart* of your loved one. Take time to be in silence, connect to the Source of love in your own heart, then imagine that person in front of you while you radiate the Presence. This is similar to praying for a sick or troubled family member or friend. It can give you clarity and respect in a situation that is challenging you. Solving problems from ego alone can be difficult. Sitting in Remembrance can profoundly connect your heart to someone, and help you see your relationship from a deeper point of view.

While listening to others, we are usually busy thinking about what to say or how to help fix their problems, rather than listening to their hearts with our heart. What we all yearn for most is to be heard. Practice the Remembrance while you are listening. Radiate Love and hold their hearts. You will be a more helpful witness to their own process, their own healing. They will feel it, believe me. Most people are not used to being heard. It is a gift to anyone when you are truly present. When you are listening in Remembrance, the Divine Presence in them often shines the light on their solution. It may not happen immediately, but the insight they receive will probably be more helpful than any advice you conjure up in your mind. You are not responsible for everyone's problems. Rely on the Love. Place your attention in your heart and connect to the heart of the person in front of you, holding it in Divine Presence. Little miracles happen. Whether you say something or not, there is a Remembrance of love, the deepest method of healing.

The Remembrance can create a ripple effect to transform our world. When babies are held in love, they blossom.

There are so many children who are crying, yearning to be heard, to be held and to feel safe. Their hearts are hurting. Their hearts need to be held.

It is worth repeating: the best time to start bonding is as soon as you know you are pregnant. Your baby's heart and soul are there, however tiny, open and ready to be loved. Remember that the mother's and baby's body are still one body. Because of this, the baby feels what mom feels. By practicing the Remembrance and being in deep relationship with the Divine in your heart, your being is speaking in the language that your baby can understand:

the language of love
the language of safety
the language of acceptance
the language of belonging

As your heart is immersed more deeply in the Name, your heart expands and envelops the precious being growing in your belly. In this way, the baby will be nurtured and will thrive, not just survive. Over time, you will feel connection to your baby even before you see his or her face. This is the ultimate foundation of parenting with a deep heart from the start.

The beauty of the process is that you are already holding your baby's heart. The spiritual and emotional contact you create with your infant is crucial from conception through your baby's first year.

Don't forget to talk to your baby. Babies understand. If you and someone else argue, reassure your baby. Say, "My little one, I was arguing, but it wasn't about you. You are safe and I love you." *The baby needs to know.*

And always return to the Remembrance.

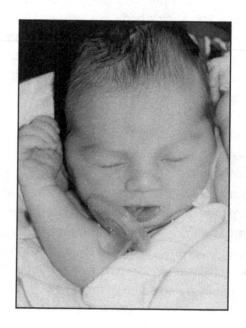

Chapter 10

Right After Birth

Those Precious First Moments

At times it is necessary to whisk a baby away for medical reasons. However, there are countless benefits to keeping your baby with you, especially if your baby is born healthy without any symptoms of stress. Babies taken away from their moms immediately after birth tend to cry. Babies who stay with their moms tend to be quiet and alert. They feel connected and safe. Keep your baby in those first precious minutes if you can.

Once dried, your baby can lie on your belly or chest. This creates more warmth than blankets do. It is best to delay the bath. Your baby relies on the smell and taste of the amniotic fluid to connect to the fluid that comes from the breast. If you intend to breast feed, allowing your baby that journey to the breast strengthens the legs and allows latching to be a natural occurrence rather than something that needs to be learned. If you postpone breast feeding until after the bath, the inherent sensing mechanism provided by nature has been washed away! Even though it may take an hour for the baby to journey from your belly to your breast, it will be much more effective than bathing the baby first, and then struggling to create the connection later. (*From Your Amazing Newborn,* by Dr. Marshall Klaus)[16]

THOSE PRECIOUS FIRST DAYS

A story in *Mothering Magazine* told of a top executive who lived on hyperdrive, who decided to give birth with the assistance of a midwife. One requirement in their contract was that the mom stay in her bedroom for the first weeks of her baby's life, without cell phones, pagers, television, nor the internet. Her friends thought she was crazy. They were also certain she wouldn't last.

The purpose behind this was to be fully present with her baby. Life became timeless as they bonded, similar to our own love stories, when all we wanted to be was *to be with our loved one, and nothing else but our beloved mattered.* She became familiar with her little girl's awareness, her cues. She was thrilled at how attentive her daughter was to her mom's voice, to her facial expressions.

Her husband fielded phone calls, did laundry, and brought her meals. In between, he joined his wife and baby to share their precious connection, lounging in the love. They experienced what was valuable, what was real. The weeks flew by. By then, they knew her cries and what they meant. They **knew who she was and what she needed.** They knew her as someone who could communicate. The gift they gave their daughter was the foundation of security and trust. In her first days of life, she knew how precious she was to them, that she was worth their time, and that they were there for her, *in her joy AND in her discomfort.* Her needs were being met in a loving way. The gift she gave to them was pure, unconditional love.[17]

The greatest investment you can make for yourself after giving birth is to retreat into your own sacred space with your newly born baby. It is such a precious time, for you to truly know your little one and touch the purest of hearts. You will be facing the essence of the love that came through you. How blessed you can be, to see that sweet soul through the window of unconditional eyes. Your baby is your mirror, to remind you who you really are, where you came from, and of your own innocence. Your connection to your baby will help you remember the truth about yourself. All babies want and need in that moment is to be in love with you. Allow yourself to receive that precious gift. It is deep spiritual medicine.

Yes, they will need to eat and be changed and much more, but in the moments after birth, give yourself the time to fall in love. Especially when you go home, nothing, absolutely nothing can be more important than getting to know your baby: not well-meaning friends, extended family, phone calls, or birth announcements. Nothing! Give yourselves a few weeks to fully receive this most precious gift. Mom, stay in your bedroom with your baby. Let the baby's father fix food and bring it to you.

This time of connection is too important to dilute with the busy outside world. The miracle of nature itself is calling you into Remembrance. What you create with your baby in those first days will deeply affect you, your baby, and the quality of your relationship for the rest of your life.

When you slow down, you will learn how your baby speaks to you. You and baby connect more deeply, making parenting a lot more meaningful. Your baby has a lot to teach you!

The child you cherish now will feel cherished in the future. You hold your future in your hands. Hold it deeply with your heart, in love. This practice will anchor your parenting in a way that withstands the outside influences of our culture, and create a healthy refuge for your whole family.

ABOUT THE BREAST FEEDING PROCESS

Mother's milk is medicinal. It is rich in nutrients, and creates higher immunity for infants. It can contribute to increasing a baby's IQ by five points, and appears to lower a mom's chances of breast cancer later in life. [18,19] Most women think that latching on should be immediate. If nursing doesn't happen before the baby is bathed, or if the baby is taken away for a while, it may take more time. The same is true if you had difficulties during the birth, are recovering from anesthesia, or are experiencing pain (or all three!).

Remember: your baby is medicine for you.

Latching on might take more time. Sometimes, moms feel overwhelmed or inadequate if results aren't immediate. Be patient. This is an organic process. Give yourself and your baby time to learn. It happens more easily when you are relaxed. If you start to feel frustrated, your baby will feel it, and get distracted. Remember. Breathe deep into those feelings. Everything happens in its own perfect timing. Let any tension created by high expectations dissipate. Once you align with the love inside you, you can focus on the miracle of your baby's journey of learning how to eat. In this way, you are fully present with your baby, not just invested in results. This helps your baby feel secure and encouraged by your acceptance and patience. You can then enjoy your baby's learning process and development. The result will be pleasurable for both of you.

ABOUT CIRCUMCISION

Circumcisions are no longer recommended by the Academy of Pediatrics if there is good hygiene. I have witnessed hundreds of circumcisions in my work as a registered nurse. Considering the awareness of infants, I feel strongly that the way the procedure is carried out is appalling.

You have read in chapter 4 about seeing life from the baby's point of view. How would you feel if someone picked you up without explaining anything, took off your clothes, strapped your legs down, then cut you, altering your body forever? Again, this is done without any warning and without telling the baby what is about to happen, except for some superfluous comment; most commonly, "*I am going to sharpen your pencil.*" ***REALLY? Could that be more barbaric, now that you know that babies remember?***

Some doctors are convinced that it doesn't hurt. Yes, they use local anesthesia, but that wears off fairly quickly. I have seen little guys sleep more, eat less, cry harder, especially when they wet their diapers. They also withdraw, and assume a deeper fetal position. This all stems from the belief that babies don't remember a thing. We now know that isn't true.

Whether I am for or against circumcision is irrelevant. The way it is done is violating. In the Jewish religion, circumcision is done in a sacred ceremony. I am certain that intention makes a big difference in the impact it has on a baby boy. If you choose to have this procedure done, do so in a conscious manner. Prepare your little boy so that he knows there will be discomfort. Tell him how it will happen. Be there with him, for him. Hold him dearly. Hold his heart in love and safety. **That** is how it should happen.

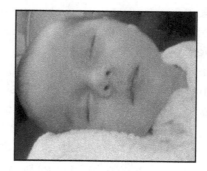

Chapter 11

Moms Who Remembered

SARAH

Sarah was excited to be pregnant with her first baby, but was plagued with morning sickness throughout her first trimester. She was always sick, and many old issues surfaced during this time. When her physical symptoms distracted her, she breathed the Name into her heart, to tune into herself. She faced her fears of inadequacy, fears of not being a good mom. The Remembrance helped her to heal old emotional patterns of her childhood. As these old feelings emerged, she trusted that she was being prepared for birth and motherhood. She realized that as she cleared away her own emotional baggage, she could indeed be a good mother.

The Remembrance also helped her to connect to her baby, especially when it was hard for her to even imagine that she really was pregnant. First she went into her heart, then she enveloped her son's heart in hers and became more peaceful. Eventually, she felt his love and joy when she sat in the stillness. By sitting in her own presence, she truly felt her baby's heart and soul. The connection between mother and child had begun.

Sarah had a health crisis in her ninth month. She developed Bell's palsy with facial paralysis. She worried about the uncertainty of her future, not to mention the future of her family as a whole. She had trouble talking, eating, smiling and blinking. She took all this to heart and prayed to be capable of a deeper surrender. With several visits to her chiropractor, her symptoms were alleviated.

Sarah planned a home birth. Her midwife advised her that the more she was at peace with her fears, the easier that the birth would progress. Sarah admitted that she received support when she needed it. Her relationship with her husband was loving and strong, both emotionally and spiritually. Her labor lasted thirteen hours. Even though it seemed difficult, she found it empowering and loving on all levels. Her son was born very present and aware from the beginning. She remains in awe of how new each day is for him in his understanding and his development. She is fed by how much love he has to give.

Sarah's message to new moms: "Every woman is capable of a natural birth, barring complications and specific conditions. It is sad to me to see women yielding to fear-based decisions and opting for the path of medicalization. I think this is very disempowering. At least attempt the natural process first. It is rewarding even if isn't easy. When you are not drugged, you are more aware and open to the realization of the miracle of life and creation. You can experience the physiology of love Itself. I wish women would believe in themselves and know that they have the inner power to deliver naturally. It is called labor for a reason. If more women listened to their hearts, their bodies, themselves, the world would be a more loving place."

ZAINA

Zaina, mother of two children, has been using the Remembrance practice for years. She wrote:

"There are many personal benefits to doing Remembrance while pregnant. It is a time of tremendous change. The Remembrance can keep you grounded and centered. Preparing for motherhood is a physically and emotionally trying time, and this internal practice can remind you of what is truly important. It can also help you to see a larger view of our world. God puts you through trying times so you can cling to Him. This reliance can be very helpful during the transformative process that changes your bodies, lifestyle and mindset.

"The birthing process involves complete surrender. Remembrance brings your focus inward, which is important at birth. It also helps you to feel embraced by the Divine. You can offer up your pain or upsetting emotions, instead of bracing yourself, being alone in it. It's more than wonderful for the baby to be born in an environment where everyone is in conscious Remembrance of the divine reality of love. This eases the baby's transition because the environment is still and joyful.

"My evolution to parenthood and multiple children has stretched me and made me grow. Many issues surfaced and I really had to let go of things, feelings and desires. I realized that all my deep heart wanted was to move closer to divine reality and truth. I experienced this intense process with less resistance when I was practicing Remembrance. It is through this continuous practice that I surrender to what my life brings.

"Another thing for me personally was to learn to ask for what I want and need, in prayer. In my parenting I have learned the importance of asking, 'Please let her sleep tonight,' or 'Please show me how I need to handle this situation.'

"I have also used the Remembrance to better hold my child's heart. Parenting issues are often very emotionally charged. We as parents still have so many ingrained influences from our parents, our childhoods, mixed with cultural biases. It is very helpful to see from the child's point of view, to look for their needs, not just our desires. The Remembrance can help filter our own desires and emotions to clarify what the child's heart is needing, what is for their highest good.

"It is easy to get caught between cultural norms, expectations, my own preferences, and what my heart wants. Doing Remembrance and feeling each decision in my heart has really helped me to follow my heart. It helps me to see the whole picture more clearly. It has enriched our lives greatly, on all levels, in all ways."

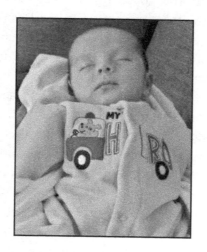

Chapter 12

Dads: What You Need to Know

Do you recall Thomas Verny's research results from Chapter 3? He found that the second most important factor that determines the baby's quality of life is how the dad relates to the mom. When your baby's mom is stressed, she produces the stress hormone cortisol, which not only constricts the mom, but also constricts the baby. When she is happy and feeling supported, her body relaxes, thereby supporting the optimal growth, development, IQ, and health of your son or daughter.

Dad, you have a very important role in keeping your family whole. You are an integral part of the team. Some dads feel left out, or feel uncertain as they see their partner transform into motherhood. Everything is changing! It has to. Remember your own heart, then hold her heart and soul in the process.

From conception until the baby is a year old, taking care of mom and taking care of the baby is one and the same thing, because they still share so much chemistry. Help your baby's mom take care of herself. For example, foot massages are mutually beneficial. You will receive as you give. Schedule quality time together to nurture your relationship and help each other through this amazing phase.

Remember that your hearts and souls are already connected to your baby's.
Creation itself brings the state of grace. Learning to hold each other's hearts will protect your relationship during tough times.

The struggle at the level of ego will be easier to release, once you experience a deeper Reality with each other. You will feel safer with each as trust builds. Your baby will communicate back the Love that you bring. You will remember that you too, you two, came from the same innocence and purity.

A bond this deep will never be broken.

We all suffer from the human condition, and fall short on a regular basis. No one is expecting you to be Mr. & Mrs. Perfect. You may remember the story how the unborn baby jumped when the parents started shouting. When there is tension between you, or an argument - these do inevitably happen - remind your baby that the argument is not about them. Babies need to know, they need to remember the situation accurately. Unless you tell them otherwise, they will think it is about them. because their world is still so egocentric. Reassurance is essential for your baby's sense of safety. The simple solution is to tell the truth. It will be recorded in the baby's cellular memory that sometimes people who love each other also disagree with each other, and that the baby is not at fault. This will maintain the baby's developing self worth, and help him or her stay connected to you, instead of withdrawing from a perceived threat. Always remember to tell your babies that they are loved, that they are safe. Take the time to give your baby the best start in life.

Communicating with your baby before birth reduces complications at birth. Helping your baby's mom reduce stress during pregnancy creates a smarter, healthier baby. Holding your baby's heart before birth creates a trusting, mentally and emotionally healthy baby. Transforming your own emotional patterns and wounds before birth frees your baby from inheriting your own unresolved issues.

REMEMBER THE MIRACLE THAT YOU ARE.

Chapter 13

It is Never Too Late

No matter how old your children are, you can start now to hold their hearts in Love. It is never to late to start remembering who you are, who they are, and to hold their hearts. Even if they are miles away, prayer is not limited by time or distance. No matter what the physical or emotional distance, there is no such thing as a heart that doesn't still truly want the love of the mother.

SPREAD THE WORD, SHARE THE LOVE

My own prayer is that you feel inspired to experience how much healing you can create. If this practice works for you, please share it with those you love.

The world needs a lot of help right now. Many hearts are hurting and people are suffering. Just remember, every person, no matter his/her track record in life, needs mercy. Every person used to be a baby full of love and joy.

With that in mind:

Hold the hearts of our leaders in your prayers, rather than holding them in hatred.

Hold the hearts of your parents in love, even if they caused you pain. In the long run, your prayers for their healing will help them, *and you.*

Your deep intention will not only enrich your life by being in service to love, but it will also help to create peace on earth.

The benefits of your remembrance surpasses time and space. The person who benefits the most from your prayer practice is you.

You can give only what you have. Contentment comes from a fullness that never empties. Be full, be well. Be happy, be grateful.

Resources

There is more for you to experience if you liked this book, or know someone who will!

You are welcomed to join the membership site that supports pregnant women - or moms in general - to hold their heart space, and to remember what is important in their family: the love that is inherent in you and your children.

If you are a grandmother, you can create a lot of healing for your whole family by healing the wounding from your past. What you heal gets passed on for generations to come.

I invite you to participate at any stage of parenting. Like I said, it is never too late to open your heart and soul.

Please visit www.yourbabyremembers.com for more information.

If you are interested in more healing techniques, visit www.healingtouchforbabies.com for more extensive workshop events.

It is time

to nurture our children,

our families,

our earth.

It starts with

ourselves.

Thanks for buying this book.

Love a mother and buy her a copy.

Endnotes

1. Thomas Verny. *The Secret Life of the Unborn Child.* Toronto: Dell Publishing, 1984, p.13
2. Verny, p. 70
3. Verny, p. 67
4. Verny, p. 20-21
5. Verny, p. 78
6. Verny, p. 80-81
7. David Chamberlain. *The Mind of Your Newborn Baby.* Berkeley, CA: North Atlantic Books, 1990, p. 88
8. Chamberlain, p. 15
9. Chamberlain, Intro, p. xxii
10. Chamberlain, p. 105
11. Chamberlain, pp. 121-124
12. Wendy McCarty. Power of Beliefs: What Babies are Teaching Us. 2002. p. 7 & 18
13. McCarty, p.14
14. Masaru Emoto. *The Hidden Messages in Water.* New York: Atria Books, 2001, p. 66
15. Emoto, p.155.
16. Marshall Klaus. *Your Amazing Newborn.*
17. Mothering Magazine. October 2007. Art of Mothering: Primal Love - The bond between mother and baby.
18. American Journal of Clinical Nutrition, Vol. 70, No. 4, 525-535, October 1999
19. The Lancet, Volume 360, Issue 9328, Pages 187 - 195, 20 July 2002

CPSIA information can be obtained
at www.ICGtesting.com
Printed in the USA
FSHW022035281019
63509FS

9 780983 474906